Succeeding With
Lit Circles

Written by Barbara Doherty and Charlotte Jaffe
Illustrated by Karen Birchak

ISBN 1-56644-128-5

© 2004 Educational Impressions, Inc.

PRINTED IN THE U.S.A.

EDUCATIONAL IMPRESSIONS, INC.
Hawthorne, New Jersey 07507

Table of Contents

Introduction

Succeeding with Lit Circles provides an easy-to-follow, step-by-step format that will help you create effective literature circles in your classroom. Lit Circles combine a skills mini-lesson, independent or small-group reading, writing, book discussions, and concluding activities that are shared by the whole class. Help your students discover the joy of reading and become life-long readers by providing an opportunity for them to participate in a classroom literature circle.

Highlights of the Book

TEACHER BOOK SELECTION
Choosing the right books for your students to read is a very important element of the unit. The Teacher Book Selection page gives you ideas for selecting and gathering the books you will need.

STUDENT BOOK SELECTION
Establish a Meet-the-Books session to familiarize students with the book choices you have made for the unit. Students then fill out Choice Sheets to help with book selection and group placement.

GROUPING
Several methods of grouping are discussed. Although there may be times when you want to have above-level readers working together in a group, heterogeneous grouping is usually recommended. Struggling readers will gain understanding and vocabulary by listening to others read and by joining in the discussions.

SOCIAL SKILLS
In order for a Lit Circle to be successful, students must follow certain basic rules appropriate for cooperative learning. Most involve common courtesy and thoughtfulness. A Social-Skills Chart is included, but students should be encouraged to add to the chart.

COMPREHENSION AND DISCUSSION QUESTIONS
Discussion is the backbone of the literature circle. Asking the correct questions enhances the enjoyment and understanding of the story. Guidelines for asking questions that promote effective discussion are explained. Students will use Lit Logs to record their reading responses and answers to questions.

PROJECTS
Project ideas, suitable for many books, are provided to help students select and create meaningful extension projects. Examples of book-specific, post-reading activities from several L-I-T *Guides*™, written by the authors and published by Educational Impressions, are also provided.

LIT-CIRCLE ROLES
Six roles that are important to the success of the literature circle are carefully explained in this section of the book. If your class is large, other roles may be added. Use the two Aesop's fables to practice the roles with your class.

CULMINATING ACTIVITIES
Story Skits, Literary Wax Museum, and Lit Bowl are exciting and effective culminating events your students will enjoy. Directions for creating them in your classroom are given in this section.

ASSESSMENT
The Teacher Record Form, Observation Form, Self-Evaluation Form, and Group-Evaluation Form are provided to help determine your students' competency. You may wish to develop other types of assessments, such as project rubrics or anecdotal records. Use the included assessments as they are presented or as a guide to help you develop your own forms.

GLOSSARY
The glossary contains a list of literary terms that can be used as the basis of mini-lessons with your students.

BIBLIOGRAPHY
Books that are well written and which contain material appropriate for Lit-Circle discussion groups are listed in the Bibliography. Separate lists are provided for Grades 3–4, Grades 5–6, and Grades 7–8.

What Are Lit Circles?

Lit Circles provide new ways of thinking about teaching reading and writing. They are small groups of students (three to six students are advisable) who get together on a regular basis to read and talk about a novel, short story, or poem with their peers. These literature circles may vary according to reading requirements, group roles, method of selecting literature, assessment techniques, and time limitations.

Within their literature circles, students have the opportunity to engage in lively discussions and share interpretations of the literature that they are reading together. Readers are encouraged to make connections between the stories that they read and their personal lives and to help each other construct meaning from the material that they are reading. By teaching the social skills of cooperative learning, the teacher can make sure that all students are able to fully participate in the literature discussions.

Choice is an important and motivating component of literature circles. Students are asked to choose the books they would like to read in their Lit Circle from among those suggested and described by the teacher. They may also choose or create their own questions to use in Lit-Circle discussions as well as decide upon the number of pages to be read at each session.

As part of the Lit-Circle process, students are given many varied opportunities to develop their higher-level, critical- and creative-thinking skills through challenging writing responses to literature and purposeful projects that are related to their reading.

Observations and anecdotal records of each student's participation in Lit-Circle discussions are often utilized in assessing the students' learning accomplishments. Group and self-evaluations that encourage students to think about their own effectiveness are also necessary evaluation tools.

Why Are Lit Circles Effective?

Lit Circles benefit students' reading development in a number of ways. Students learn to respond to open-ended questions, to make inferences, to connect ideas, and to make predictions. They also gain an understanding of literary devices, enhance their vocabularies, and improve their comprehension skills. In addition, students engage in cooperative-learning opportunities that provide the foundation for the development of social-interaction skills. Through Lit-Circle discussions, students will greatly improve their skills in oral communication by talking about the story and voicing opinions in a logical context.

By participating in active reading experiences such as literature circles, students are more motivated to read and are more able to retain what they have read. Their understanding of the reading material is enhanced. Because students are exposed to varying opinions and perspectives during group-discussion periods, their ability to think critically is expanded. By working in small groups, students develop more self-confidence about contributing an idea or offering an opinion, and there are more opportunities for every student to participate fully in the literature-circle discussion. More-able readers act as peer mentors by modeling the skill of reading with fluency and expression.

Literature circles are an important part of a balanced literacy program, which should also include modeled reading, shared reading, guided reading, independent reading, modeled writing, shared writing, interactive writing, guided writing, and independent writing. During the process of literature circles, students are given many opportunities to be involved in activities at the different levels of balanced literacy.

Getting Started

Before beginning a Lit-Circle program in your classroom, take time to do the following:

- Develop social-behavior guidelines for your students to follow. A sample Social Behavior Chart is provided for your convenience. Have the students add their contributions to the list. Enlarge the chart and display it in your classroom.

- Decide how you will group your students. If necessary, create a plan to help struggling readers improve their skills so that they can fully participate in the Lit Circle. Suggestions are provided.

- Familiarize your students with story elements such as setting, characterization, plot, climax, and resolution. Show them how to make connections between the story and other subject areas, other books, and personal experiences.

- Explain and demonstrate questioning strategies and how to respond to them. Model open discussions that include both questions and responses with the whole class. Make sure that students understand that there may be more than one correct answer to an open-ended question.

- Model each of the roles that students will be using in their Lit-Circle discussion groups. These roles are described in detail. Plan to have the whole class experience each of the roles. Use a short story that all the students have read or the fable samples provided in this book.

- Explain the requirements for extension projects. Show samples of projects that meet your expectations. Review the Pick-a-Project activities with your students.

- Guide students in the use and creation of a Lit Log. A sample entry and instructions are included. Lit Logs are used to record responses to discussion questions. These responses should be written in complete sentences and should include details to support them. Students may also use the Lit Logs to record other responses to their reading, such as book reviews, point-of-view articles, reflections on the story, vocabulary activities, personal connections, and questions to discuss during Lit-Circle time. Lit Logs can be made from composition books, folders, or loose-leaf binders or they can be created on the computer.

Preparation Strategies

The following are suggestions for preparing your classroom for Lit Circles.

- Arrange desks, tables, and chairs in a way that will allow your students to move about the room easily. One possibility is to arrange four to six student desks into a group to form a table. Another is to create a cozy area of the room by using carpeting, beanbag chairs, cushions, etc. Groups can take turns using this special area.

- Keep ample supplies of dictionaries, tablets, pens, pencils, markers, and sticky notes on hand. Also be sure your Lit Logs, book copies, and student folders are readily and easily accessible.

- Create a separate supply center for students working on projects. Include varieties of tagboard, multi-colored construction paper, glue sticks, scissors, and scraps. Make copies of the Pick-a-Project pages to be kept in this area.

- Decide on a system for material retrieval and distribution. You might delegate this responsibility to one person in each group.

- Create a Lit Log for each student. This can be a marble composition book, a spiral notebook, or a teacher-made booklet. For example, you might staple a series of papers together with a cover made from construction paper. The Lit Log should be labeled with the book title and student's name.

- Make a folder for each student's work. You might want to use colored folders available in office supply stores. Decorate the covers with an illustration that represents the story. Label the cover with the title and the student's name. Use the folder to keep the student's Lit Log, question sheets, activity sheets, mini-lesson pages, and sticky notes.

Materials Checklist

Use the following checklist to determine which resources you already have and which you need to gather before beginning your Lit Circles. You may also want to note who is responsible for providing each item.

Item   ## Person Responsible

Pocket Folders   _____

Storage Crates (Baskets, Containers)   _____

Cushions, Carpeting, Etc.   _____

Markers: _____ Sets   _____

Pens and Pencils for Each Table   _____

Pads of Sticky Notes   _____

Dictionaries   _____

Choice Sheets   _____

Project Planning Sheets   _____

Lit Logs   _____

Role Sheets   _____

Specific Activity Pages:

_____   _____

_____   _____

_____   _____

Other Supplies:

_____   _____

_____   _____

Multiple Copies of the Chosen Titles:

_____   _____

_____   _____

_____   _____

© *Educational Impressions, Inc.*

Lit-Circle Models

Lit Circles in the classroom may vary in form. Two popular models are summarized below. The difference between these two models is in the formation of the questions to be used during the discussion period. (See Step 10.)

MODEL #1

Note: The order of the steps may be changed as desired. Each step is explained in more detail throughout the book.

STEP 1: SOCIAL SKILLS
The teacher reviews the social skills necessary for a successful Lit-Circle experience. Several skills are listed on the Social Skills sheet. Students should be encouraged to add to the list.

STEP 2: TEACHER BOOK SELECTION
The teacher selects books for the Lit-Circle unit based upon classroom needs.

STEP 3: STUDENT BOOK SELECTION
Students use the Choice Sheets to make selections unless everyone is reading the same book.

STEP 4: GROUPING
The teacher groups the students into workable Lit Circles.

STEP 5: PRE-READING LESSON
Provide background to make sure that all students have the necessary basic knowledge for the chosen selection.

STEP 6: MINI-LESSONS
Mini-lessons may be taught to the entire class or to small groups according to need.

STEP 7: LIT-CIRCLE ROLES
The teacher reviews the responsibilities that accompany the various Lit-Circle roles. Students should practice the roles as an entire class. Before the start of each Lit Circle, these roles are assigned by the teacher or chosen by group members.

STEP 8: QUESTIONING TECHNIQUES
Be sure students know how to have a discussion and how to formulate good questions and follow-up questions.

STEP 9: READING TIMES
Students read for the assigned time. (Reading may also be assigned as homework.) Students make notes in their Lit Logs as they read in preparation for discussion. Those who finish ahead of time should be directed to work on a project from the Pick-a-Project section.

STEP 10: LIT-CIRCLE DISCUSSION
The Discussion Leader determines the main discussion questions and provides the follow-up questions. Other members of the group may also contribute questions and follow-up questions.

STEP 11: DEBRIEFING

Debriefing takes place with the entire class. If a book being discussed has not been introduced in a Meet-the-Books session, the story should be summarized and enough information presented so that members of the other groups have basic knowledge about the book. Groups will share their experiences. The teacher may ask leading questions regarding literary techniques, behavior, connections to other classroom subjects, personal experiences, and so on.

STEP 12: ASSESSMENT

Assessment is ongoing and varied and includes observations, checklists, group evaluations, quizzes, teacher-made rubrics, and self-evaluations.

MODEL #2

STEPS 1 THROUGH 9
Follow Model #1.

STEP 10: LIT-CIRCLE DISCUSSION

The teacher provides general prompts or prompts specific to the story being discussed. Students are responsible for providing follow-up questions for their groups. (Note: In this model, L-I-T *Guides*™ and other prepared guides are useful sources of questions.)

EXAMPLE OF GENERAL PROMPT:
The teacher might write the following on the board:
    What did _____ do that surprised you?

Students might follow up with the following:
    Have you ever done anything like that?
    Would _____ make a good friend? Why or why not?

EXAMPLE OF SPECIFIC PROMPT:
The teacher might write the following on the board for a Lit Circle discussing *Bridge to Terabithia:*
    In *Bridge to Terabithia,* Jess feels like a coward. Do you agree that he was a coward, or do you think that he was wise not to take a risk?

STEP 11: DEBRIEFING
Follow Model #1.

STEP 12: ASSESSMENT
Follow Model #1.

GOAL: Independence

In any model, the goal is for students eventually to become independent! The teacher becomes a facilitator. After completing a few Lit-Circle experiences, many teachers develop hybrid versions that fit their particular needs and constraints.

Social Skills

In order to have a successful Lit-Circle experience, it is crucial that all participants follow cooperative-learning rules. Most of these rules involve common courtesy. The Social-Skills Chart on the following page may be enlarged and displayed in your classroom. Have students brainstorm and add any other rules they deem necessary. If you prefer, you can have the list completely created by the students. Elicit any responses that are lacking that you feel are important.

Lit Circles Social-Skills Chart

★   Use quiet voices during discussion time.

★   Allow only one speaker at a time.

★   Stay on the topic.

★   Explain your reasoning.

★   Respect the ideas and opinions of other students.

★   Be a good listener.

★   Do not allow one student to dominate the discussion.

★   Encourage everyone to join in the discussion.

★   Complete your group-role responsibility on time.

★   _____

★   _____

★   _____

★   _____

★   _____

★   _____

Teacher Book Selection

Choosing the right books to use in Lit Circles is crucial. Here are some tips to help you successfully select books for your class. At times you may want the entire class to read the same selection in order to satisfy curriculum requirements, to model literary techniques, or to demonstrate the Lit-Circle process.

- Consider using a particular theme that may correlate with study in another content area. Examples are events, such as the Revolutionary War; time periods, such as the Middle Ages; science topics, such as the environment; and particular culture areas, such as South America. If you decide to use the theme approach, the entire class does not have to read the same book. Choose multiple copies of a variety of titles that relate to your main theme for use with different groups.

- Gather high-quality reading materials that have recognizable literary merit.

- Try to select books that will provide opportunities for lively and meaningful discussion to take place.

- Choose books that provide examples of diversity.

- Match the readability levels of the books to your students' reading levels.

- Be sure to read the books ahead of time yourself in order to discuss the vocabulary, to prepare specific questions, to discover any controversial material, and to prepare to answer students' questions pertaining to the book.

- Acquire books from various sources:
    Ask your school media teacher for copies of books.
    Share book sets with other teachers.
    Borrow books from local or county libraries.
    Use PTA funds to purchase new books.
    Obtain bonus points from commercial book orders.
    Look in discount book stores for bargain-priced reading materials.
    Have parents and friends look for titles you need at library book sales, yard sales, tag sales, and so on.

- Review bibliographies and book lists for recommended, appropriate books your students would enjoy reading. (See the bibliographies at the end of this book.)

Student Book Selection
MEET THE BOOKS

For some Lit-Circle reading units, you may want to select the same book for your students to read in their small groups. At other times, you will want to allow students to choose the books that they will read. You may design a Lit-Circle unit around a particular theme or content area using more than one title. Students must be guided to make good choices. You can help by holding a Meet-the-Books session to introduce students to the books that will be available for the upcoming unit.

STEP 1
Provide a short introduction to the book. Give them some basic information about the setting, main characters, and theme. Highlight interesting parts, but do not reveal so much of the plot that you spoil the reading experience!

STEP 2
Explain to the students why the book is worthwhile to read. If it has won any important awards, let the students know this fact.

STEP 3
Read aloud a small portion of the book. Repeat steps 1 through 3 for each book.

STEP 4
Allow time for your students to take the books back to their desks and read a portion of the first chapters independently. This will help them judge if the books are too easy or too difficult for them to read and whether or not they interest them.

STEP 5
Instruct students not to base their choice on the length of the book, but on its quality and readability.

STEP 6
Provide the students with Choice Sheets (a sample follows). Make copies of the Choice Sheet and distribute them to your students to help in the formation of Lit-Circle groups. Five spaces are provided for writing choices.

STEP 7
After the students have filled out the sheets, collect the sheets and evaluate the choices they have requested.

STEP 8
If possible, try to give students their first or second book choice. Carefully consider the dynamics of the group before placing a student in it. Make sure that the group is balanced and can work together effectively.

Book Selection

CHOICE SHEET

_____
(STUDENT NAME)

Book Titles in Order of Preference:

1.

2.

3.

4.

5.

Pre-Reading Activities

After deciding on the book to be read, provide the group with background information and some pre-reading or "warm-up" activities. In addition to increasing interest, this will assist in making the Lit Circle a successful experience for your students.

- Provide students with information regarding the author and, if applicable, the illustrator.

- Provide an overview that will increase interest in reading the story.

- Provide students with a map and discuss the location of the setting.

- Provide cultural and historical background for the story.

- Provide students with information regarding the theme or topic.

- Read another book or article or watch a video on the same topic.

- Ask students leading questions about one of the problems a character in the story encounters.

- Supply information concerning an event or item that has an important part in the story.

- Sample a particular food item of the culture.

- Invite a speaker who has a connection with the topic or theme.

- Make a craft or learn a song or dance of the specific time period and/or culture.

- Introduce any examples of strange dialect, colloquialisms, or words whose meanings have changed with time.

- If there is specialized vocabulary, provide some of the basics, including definitions.

- Have students make predictions about the plot.

NOTE: On the following pages are examples of specific pre-reading activities that refer to particular works of children's literature. They are taken from the L-I-T *Guide*™ Series, written by the authors and published by Educational Impressions, Inc.

Sample Pre-Reading Activities

*The following pre-reading activities are specific to works of popular children's literature.

From the L-I-T *Guide*™ for *Bridge to Terabithia,*
by Katherine Paterson
Pre-Reading Activity
Colloquialisms

In rural Virginia, where this story takes place, many local expressions, or colloquialisms, are used. This practice is found in other parts of the United States as well. Depending upon the region in which you live, a bag might be referred to as a sack, soda as pop, a tadpole as a polliwog, trash as rubbish, or ashes as cinders. The large sandwich consisting of a long split roll containing a variety of fillings might be called a hero, a hoagie, a grinder, or a submarine sandwich! In some parts of the United States, pizza is referred to as a tomato pie.

In addition to the differences in word choices to describe the same thing, regional pronunciations also may differ. For example, in New England the word "northeaster" is pronounced "nor'easter" and is used to describe a storm or gale from the northeast. The word "park" is pronounced "paak" and "chowder" is pronounced "chow-dah."

What local expressions, or colloquialisms, are common where you live? Think of items of clothing, games, weather conditions, parts of your home, and foods. Have fun!

From the L-I-T *Guide*™ for *Roll of Thunder, Hear My Cry,*
by Mildred Taylor
Pre-Reading Information
Tenant Farming and Sharecropping

When the Civil War ended, many planters did not have the money to hire farm laborers; therefore, they began to sell portions of their land. In time, a very small number of freed slaves were able to acquire small farms. A few others—like many poor whites—entered into a relationship known as tenant farming. In a tenant relationship, the planter rented portions of his land to a number of tenants, who paid their rent in the form of a share of their crop—usually one fourth to one third. The tenants provided their own seed, tools, and other supplies. Some tenant farmers eventually managed to save enough money to buy their own plot of land.

Related to tenant farming was sharecropping. Most sharecroppers were blacks. Sharecroppers provided the labor; they were given a cabin, seed, tools, and a mule and were expected to work the land for the planter. In return, the sharecroppers were paid, but not until harvest time; therefore, they were forced to buy their food and other provisions on credit. Most of their share of the crop went to pay back the loans and the interest that accumulated. In many cases the same person who owned the farm also owned the store at which the sharecroppers were expected to shop. The landowner/shopkeeper became an important figure in the economy of the South.

*The activities in this section were taken from the L-I-T *Guide*™ Series, written by the authors and published by Educational Impressions, Inc.

From the L-I-T *Guide*™ for *Sing Down the Moon*,
by Scott O'Dell
Pre-Reading Activity
Geographic Landforms

The opening chapters of *Sing Down the Moon* refer to many different types of landforms. These same terms are used throughout the story. With members of your group, find the definition for each term. You might have to refer to your social-studies or geography text as well as the dictionary. Create a bulletin board or table-top display of the terms. You may cut photographs from magazines, create original pictures or models, or use a combination of both for your display.

barranca	canyon	draw	gully	ledge	lowlands	meadow
	mesa	plain	ravine	ridge	valley	

From the L-I-T *Guide*™ for *The Door in the Wall*,
by Marguerite de Angeli
Pre-Reading Information
The Middle Ages: 400–1550

During much of the Middle Ages, Europe was poor, undeveloped, and sparsely populated. Forests and swamps permitted only about half the land to be farmed. War, disease, and famine kept the population low. In fact, the average life expectancy was only about thirty years! Most people did not travel, and there was little communication between cities, settlements, or villages.

Life during these centuries centered around the use of land. Usually, the land was controlled by a powerful lord with his knights and foot soldiers. It was farmed by his peasants. These workers grew and gathered the crops, raised the domestic food-animals, etc. In return, the peasants were granted refuge in the castle during times of pestilence and war.

Life for the lords, ladies, and knights was more interesting. They feasted in the castle and often were entertained by wandering minstrels.

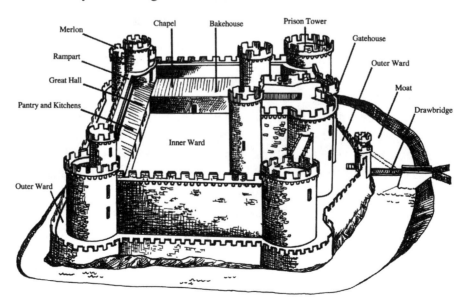

Grouping

Although there may be times when you want to have above-level readers working together, heterogeneous grouping is usually recommended. The team approach allows less-able readers to be successful with books of any length while benefitting more-able readers as well. Comprehension skills and vocabulary development of all students are enriched by the Lit-Circle experience. Students with varied experiences add to the diversity of the discussions, and all participants gain by seeing things from varying points of view. Each member of the group benefits by discussing and responding to the material and by piggybacking off the ideas of others.

METHODS
There are several methods that may be used to group your students for Lit Circles. Keep in mind that groups are fluid. Based on your observations of group dynamics, you may regroup for the maximum benefit of the entire class. After completing a reading selection, reorganize your students for the next Lit-Circle experience.

Random Grouping
Random grouping can be accomplished by having students pick the numbers 1 to 4, etc., out of a box. All those with the same number become a group. (Note: The numbers will vary depending upon the number of groups you will have.)

Teacher-Directed Grouping
The teacher may choose group members based on observations. At different times, different qualities will be used. A few possibilities are gender (same or mixed), reading abilities, personalities, and class status. Be aware of students with strong personalities and of students who do not seem to get along well together.

Student-Choice Grouping
If you want to involve students in the formation of Lit-Circle groups, ask them to complete a card on which they name three students with whom they wish to be grouped. Within reason, attempt to fulfill these requests. Friends sometimes work well together; however, it is important to encourage different groupings.

Book-Selection Grouping
Students can be grouped by reading interest. Ask them to complete the Choice Sheet on which they list the books they would like to read in order of preference. Within reason, attempt to fulfill these requests. Those students who do not get their first or second choice should be given their first choice the next time.

STUDENTS UNABLE TO WORK IN A GROUP SETTING
For varying reasons a student may be unable to work in a group setting. Talk to that student to ascertain the reason and to determine if the problem can be easily resolved. If necessary, give him or her a choice each day of working alone or in a group. As a last resort, allow the student to work alone and to complete the activities independently. You must use your best judgment in determining what will be most successful for all of your students.

Adjustments for At-Risk Readers

GENERAL SUGGESTIONS

- Use a few sentences to summarize each chapter describing the plot development.

- Arrange for another person to pre-read the selection to or with the student: another student, a classroom aide, a family member, or other volunteer.

- Create a character sketch for each of the main characters. Identify the villain, the hero, the heroine, the parents of a character, etc.

- Complete a graphic-organizer form with the student. Show the characters' relationships to one another.

- Tape the story, allowing the student to listen to the story while reading the text.

- Co-read the story with the student.

- Permit the student to read with *you* and to join the *group* for discussion and follow-up activities.

ADDITIONAL SUGGESTIONS FOR WORKING WITH E.S.L. STUDENTS

- Seek assistance from someone who speaks the student's primary language. This might be a member of the student's family, a community member, a teacher, or another student.

- Look for editions of the story in the student's primary language. Allow the student to answer by drawing when applicable if his or her written English language vocabulary is limited.

Lit-Circle Roles

There are six roles that should be a part of most Lit Circles: Discussion Leader, Passage Perfecter, Vocabulary Detective, Creative Connector, Character Coordinator, and Story Sketcher. Students should rotate roles with each new Lit-Circle assignment. If the Lit Circle comprises less than six students, eliminate one or two roles or ask some of the students to take more than one role. Roles may also be added as necessary; two possible additional roles are Story Map Maker, who shows plot sequence, and Setting Supervisor, who describes changes in the story's setting.

It is important to thoroughly review the roles and their accompanying responsibilities before beginning the Lit Circle. Role Sheets are valuable in helping students take notes as they read in order to prepare for the Lit-Circle discussion. With the information in front of them, they are able to contribute more fully during the discussions. Copy and distribute the sheets as necessary. Instruct students to use extra sheets of paper as needed.

Although the role of leader is generally present in every discussion, the teacher does not have to use the other roles every time students gather in their Lit Circles. As students become more experienced, they are able to use varied responses in the discussion without being specifically assigned to roles.

ROLES

- Discussion Leader -

- Passage Perfecter -

- Vocabulary Detective -

- Creative Connector -

- Character Coordinator -

- Story Sketcher -

Role Sheet
DISCUSSION LEADER

The Discussion Leader is given the task of creating thought-provoking questions to use in leading the Lit-Circle discussion. The leader is also responsible for directing the follow-up questioning and comment from the group. The Discussion Leader must make sure that the discussion runs smoothly and that all members of the group participate equally.

NOTE: In Model #2, the teacher provides the questions and the group creates the follow-up questions to use in the discussion; however, the Discussion Leader is still in charge of conducting the discussion.

◆◆

Discussion Leader's Response

After reading the assigned material, create five questions that can be used in the Lit-Circle discussion. Try to use interpretive, open-ended questions that will evoke the most discussion. Refer to the Bloom's Taxonomy Chart if necessary. Avoid questions that elicit "yes" and "no" responses.

1.

2.

3.

4.

5.

◆◆

Lit Circle Tips

1. Make sure to ask only one question at a time. Do not move on to the next question until all group members have responded.

2. Do not allow any one group member to control the discussion. If a member is monopolizing the discussion, politely ask that student to give the others a chance to voice their thoughts.

3. Encourage the group members to ask follow-up questions or to come up with questions of their own that fit in with the discussion of the reading.

Role Sheet
PASSAGE PERFECTER

The Passage Perfecter carefully identifies and selects important, humorous, unusual, interesting, confusing, or provocative well-written phrases or parts of paragraphs from the story to use in Lit-Circle discussions.

◆◆◆

Passage Perfecter's Response

List your selections and indicate the reason for your choice. Be sure to include the page numbers where the passage was found. If a selection you have chosen is long, you may write only the first and last sentences on the sheet.

PASSAGE #1: Found on page _____

_____

_____

Reason for choice: _____

PASSAGE #2: Found on page _____

_____

_____

Reason for choice: _____

PASSAGE #3: Found on page _____

_____

_____

Reason for choice: _____

•••

Lit Circle Tips

1. Evaluate your selections and share your favorite passage first.

2. Have the group discuss the meaning or importance of the selection to the story.

3. Discuss your reason for choosing the passage or phrase.

Role Sheet
VOCABULARY DETECTIVE

The Vocabulary Detective searches for words that are challenging, enriching, unusual, or interesting and defines them for the group.

◆ ◆

Vocabulary Detective's Response

When you find a word that you would like to share with your Lit Circle, write it down in the column on the left. Note the page number where the word is found in the second column. Write the meaning of the word as it is used in the passage in the third column. If you are not sure of the exact definition, use a dictionary.

WORD	PAGE	DEFINITION
_____	____	_____
_____	____	_____
_____	____	_____
_____	____	_____
_____	____	_____
_____	____	_____
_____	____	_____

◆ ◆

Lit Circle Tips

For each word…

1. Share your word orally with your group members.

2. Discuss its meaning and use in the sentence.

3. Explain your reason for selecting the word.

4. Ask your group members to use the word in an original sentence and to share the sentence with the class.

Role Sheet
CREATIVE CONNECTOR

The Creative Connector is able to make credible connections between ideas, characters, settings, and problems in the reading selection and in real life. Connections may also be made to other books that have a similar theme.

◆◆◆

Creative Connector's Response

Describe your connection in the space below. Then list the words, sentences, or phrases from the story that inspired your connection idea. You may make more than one connection if time permits.

CONNECTION #1

_____

_____

_____

_____

_____

CONNECTION #2

_____

_____

_____

_____

_____

◆◆◆

Lit Circle Tips

1. Read your connection ideas orally to your group members.

2. Allow the group members to comment on your ideas and to express their own connections to the story.

Role Sheet
CHARACTER COORDINATOR

The Character Coordinator compares and contrasts character development, identifies special character traits, and discusses relationships between characters in the story.

◆◆

Character Coordinator's Response

Write the name of each character that you wish to discuss on the line. Below it write a fact or impression about that character. For example, the White Witch in *The Lion, the Witch, and the Wardrobe* might be described as tyrannical and evil. On the other hand, Aslan might be described as brave and caring. Use the facts and impressions in your list to spark your group's discussion of the story characters.

Character#1: _____

_____

_____

Character#2: _____

_____

_____

Character#3: _____

_____

_____

◆◆

Lit Circle Tips

1. Present your list of character comparisons and contrasts to the group.

2. Ask the group members if they agree or disagree with your assessment of the characters and why. Encourage all responses.

3. Discuss the ways in which the characters change during the story.

4. Ask group members to name specific character traits and to discuss how these traits influenced the plot development.

Role Sheet
STORY SKETCHER

The Story Sketcher sketches impressions of the story characters, events, or ideas. Pencils, crayons, markers, and other art supplies at hand can be used.

◆◆

Story Sketcher's Response

Create your sketch or sketches in the space below.

◆◆

Lit Circle Tips

1. Show your illustration(s) to your group.

2. Use your sketch(es) to elicit discussion. Allow questions and comments.

3. Explain your reason for creating each sketch.

Role-Playing Activities
AESOP'S FABLES

TO THE TEACHER

In order to help your students learn how to work independently in their Lit Circles, you must first model the process with the whole class.

For each fable…

- Copy the summary page and distribute the copies to your students.

- Ask your students to read the story silently. Then have one of the students read it aloud. (This is important if you have students who are struggling readers or ESL.)

- Assign the various roles to the students. Copy the role sheets and distribute them to the students. Because the fables are to be used by the whole class as a group, each role will be assigned to more than one student. Make sure that each role is assigned.

- Once the roles have been assigned, ask students to read the fable again independently, keeping in mind their roles as they jot down information or sketch pictures.

- Have students practice their roles using the fable. Examples are given for each role.

- Responses should be given orally with the whole class participating.

- Make sure that every student understands how to do every role.

Role-Playing Activities
AESOP'S FABLES: The Shepherd Boy & the Wolf

SUMMARY

A young shepherd boy tended his master's sheep near a dark forest which was not far from his village. It was a somewhat lonely job, and he soon became bored. One day he devised a plan to amuse himself. His master had told him to call for help if he saw a wolf attack any of the sheep in the field. The boy thought it would be fun to pretend that he saw a wolf, so he ran toward the village shouting, "Wolf! Wolf!"

The concerned villagers quickly ran out to help him, only to learn that they had been fooled. This gave the shepherd boy pleasure, and he tried the trick again a few days later. Once more the villagers came out to help them and once again they did not see a wolf near the sheep.

The following week, just as the sun was setting, a wolf really did come into the forest. It started moving in the direction of the sheep. The terrified boy cried, "Wolf! Wolf!" as loudly as he could. But this time the villagers, who had been fooled twice before, thought that the boy was again lying to them. No one came to help the shepherd boy, and many of the sheep were killed by the wolf. A village man said, "Liars are not believed, even when they are telling the truth!"

Role-Playing Activities
AESOP'S FABLE: The Shepherd Boy & the Wolf

DISCUSSION LEADER: Creates thought-provoking questions and follow-up questions.

SAMPLE QUESTION #1
Why did the shepherd boy tell lies?

Possible Answer
He was bored and he thought practical jokes were funny. The boy did not think about the possible consequences of his actions.

Possible Follow-up Questions (Answers will vary.)
What happens when you tell a lie?
Was his plan a good one? Why or why not?

SAMPLE QUESTION #2
Why didn't the villagers run to help the boy when the wolf really was present?

Possible Answer
They thought he was lying again. They did not want to make fools of themselves or waste their time by running to his aid again.

Possible Follow-up Questions (Answers will vary.)
In your opinion, were the villagers uncaring? Why or why not?
How do you think the shepherd boy felt when no one came to his aid?

SAMPLE QUESTION #3
What would you have done if you were a villager and heard the boy's cries for help the third time?

Possible Answer
These answers will vary.

Possible Follow-up Questions (Answers will vary.)
Why would you have acted in this way?
Have you ever been in a similar situation?

Role-Playing Activities
AESOP'S FABLE: The Shepherd Boy & the Wolf

PASSAGE PERFECTER: Identifies and selects important, humorous, unusual, interesting, confusing, or provocative well-written phrases or parts of paragraphs from the story.

SAMPLE PASSAGE: Found in last line of the story
A village man said, "Liars are not believed, even when they are telling the truth!"

POSSIBLE EXPLANATION
The Passage Perfecter might explain that he or she chose this passage because it is the theme of the story. He or she might elicit from the others that this is the moral of the story.

The Passage Perfecter might ask the class to discuss the meaning of this statement and its relationship to the events of the story.

Role-Playing Activities
AESOP'S FABLE: The Shepherd Boy & the Wolf

VOCABULARY DETECTIVE: Searches for words that are challenging, enriching, unusual, or interesting and defines them for the group.

SAMPLE VOCABULARY ENTRIES

WORD	PARAGRAPH	DEFINITION
devised	1	planned, created in the mind
tended	1	looked after, took care of
concerned	2	anxious, troubled
terrified	3	very frightened

POSSIBLE EXPLANATION

The word *terrified* is a vivid vocabulary word and it exactly describes the way the boy felt when he saw the real wolf approaching the sheep. The words *tended, concerned,* and *devised* are all strong, colorful verbs that help to make writing lively and interesting.

Role-Playing Activities
AESOP'S FABLE: The Shepherd Boy & the Wolf

Creative Connector: Makes credible connections between ideas, characters, settings, and problems in the reading selection and in real life. Connections may also be made to other books that have a similar theme.

EXAMPLES

The Creative Connector might describe a personal experience in which he or she told a lie and then got in trouble for doing so.

The Creative Connector might describe a personal experience in which someone else did the lying.

He or she might remember another book in which a character lies.

He or she might ask others if they ever had a similar experience, either as the person doing the lying or the person being deceived.

Role-Playing Activities
AESOP'S FABLE: The Shepherd Boy & the Wolf

Character Coordinator: Compares and contrasts character development, identifies special character traits, and discusses relationships between characters in the story.

POSSIBLE RESPONSES

Comparison of Character Traits
The shepherd boy was self-centered and cared only about his amusement. It did not matter to him that he was inconveniencing or worrying others. He was irresponsible and did not take his responsibilities seriously. Because of his behavior, several sheep were killed.

The villagers were responsible people. They came to help immediately when they thought they were needed.

The Villagers: How They Change
The villagers were very responsive the first two times the shepherd boy called for help. Later in the story, the villagers remembered that they had been tricked and did not respond.

How Character Traits Influence Plot Development
If the shepherd boy had been honest, the entire story plot would be different. The villagers would have responded when he needed help.

Role-Playing Activities
AESOP'S FABLE: The Shepherd Boy & the Wolf

Story Sketcher: Sketches impressions of the story characters, events, or ideas. Pencils, crayons, markers, and other art supplies at hand can be used.

POSSIBLE SKETCHES

The Story Sketcher might sketch a picture of the shepherd boy sitting near a forest watching the sheep.

The Story Sketcher might sketch a picture of the shepherd boy running through the village shouting, "Wolf! Wolf!"

The Story Sketcher might sketch a picture of the villagers running to his aid.

The Story Sketcher might sketch a picture of the terrified boy when the villagers do not answer his cry for help.

POSSIBLE EXPLANATIONS

The picture represents the main idea of the story.

The picture represents a humorous or unusual part of the story.

The picture represents a memorable part of the story.

The picture represents a part of the story that makes the reader happy, sad, frightened, etc.

The picture represents a clue to what will happen in the future or to what has happened in the past.

The picture represents something important to one of the characters.

Role-Playing Activities
AESOP'S FABLE: A Bundle of Sticks

SUMMARY

Long ago there lived a father who had four quarrelsome sons. The boys could not get along with each other, and that made the old man very sad. One day he decided to do something to solve the problem. First he gathered a bundle of sticks. Then he tied them together tightly and handed them to each of his sons. "Try to break the bundle," he said. But although each son tried hard, none of them was able to break the sturdy bundle of sticks.

Then the father untied the sticks and told his sons to break the sticks one by one. This proved to be a much easier task to complete, and soon all the sticks were broken. Finally, the father said to his sons, "If you all stick together, you will stand strong against your enemies. But if you do not cooperate with one another and support each other, your strength will be divided just like that of the sticks."

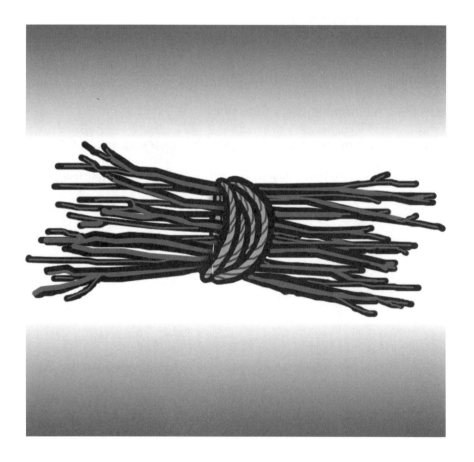

Role-Playing Activities
AESOP'S FABLE: A Bundle of Sticks

DISCUSSION LEADER: Creates thought-provoking questions and follow-up questions.

SAMPLE QUESTION #1
Why did the father decide to teach his sons a lesson?

Possible Answer
The father was upset because his sons did not get along well together.

Possible Follow-up Questions (Answers will vary.)
How have your parents tried to teach you to cooperate with your siblings and/or friends? Were they successful?

SAMPLE QUESTION #2
How did the father prove to his sons that it is important to stick together?

Possible Answer
The father asked his sons to try to break a bundle of sticks, but they could not do it. When he untied the sticks, they easily broke them one by one. He told his sons that if they did not stick together, their strength would be diminished just like that of the sticks.

Possible Follow-up Questions (Answers will vary.)
Why is it important to stick together? Can you think of any times when people should not stick together? Explain.

SAMPLE QUESTION #3
What lesson have you learned from reading this story that could be applied to your own life as a citizen of the community and of the nation?

Possible Answer
These answers will vary.

Possible Follow-up Questions (Answers will vary.)
What examples from current events or history relate to this story?

Role-Playing Activities
AESOP'S FABLE: A Bundle of Sticks

PASSAGE PERFECTER: Identifies and selects important, humorous, unusual, interesting, confusing, or provocative well-written phrases or parts of paragraphs from the story.

SAMPLE PASSAGE: Found in second paragraph of the story

The father said to his sons, "If you all stick together, you will stand strong against your enemies. But if you do not cooperate with one another and support each other, your strength will be divided just like that of the sticks."

The Passage Perfecter might discuss his or her reasons for choosing the passage.

The Passage Perfecter might ask the class to discuss the meaning of this statement and its relationship to the events of the story.

The Passage Perfecter might elicit from the others that this is the moral of the story.

Role-Playing Activities
AESOP'S FABLE: A Bundle of Sticks

VOCABULARY DETECTIVE: Searches for words that are challenging, enriching, unusual, or interesting and defines them for the group.

SAMPLE VOCABULARY ENTRIES

WORD	PARAGRAPH	DEFINITION
quarrelsome	1	tending to argue
sturdy	1	substantially built, strong
task	2	chore, job to be performed

POSSIBLE EXPLANATION

The word *quarrelsome* is a colorful adjective that perfectly describes the way the sons always argued with one another. *Sturdy* is also a good descriptive adjective; it helps the reader realize that the bundle of sticks was difficult to break. *Task* is a good word because it is not used as frequently as *chore* or *job* and it is good to use word variety in writing.

Role-Playing Activities
AESOP'S FABLE: A Bundle of Sticks

Creative Connector: Makes credible connections between ideas, characters, settings, and problems in the reading selection and in real life. Connections may also be made to other books that have a similar theme.

EXAMPLES

The Creative Connector might describe a time when he or she was a member of a team and the team succeeded because all members performed their roles well and worked together toward a common goal.

The Creative Connector might describe a time when he or she was a member of a team and the team did not succeed because all members did not perform their roles well and did not work together toward a common goal.

Role-Playing Activities
AESOP'S FABLE: A Bundle of Sticks

Character Coordinator: Compares and contrasts character development, identifies special character traits, and discusses relationships between characters in the story.

POSSIBLE RESPONSES

Comparison of Character Traits

The sons did not get along. The father wanted them to get along and to be helpful to one another.

The father was a wise man who found a simple way to teach his sons an important lesson about cooperation.

Character Development

The father starts out unhappy. He decides to do something about his problem in order to better his situation.

How Character Traits Influence Plot Development

Father was smart and resourceful. He devised an effective lesson for his sons. If he had not found a way to teach his sons a lesson, they would have continued to argue and bicker all the time. They would not have learned the importance of "sticking together."

Role-Playing Activities
AESOP'S FABLE: A Bundle of Sticks

Story Sketcher: Sketches impressions of the story characters, events, or ideas. Pencils, crayons, markers, and other art supplies at hand can be used.

POSSIBLE SKETCHES

The Story Sketcher might sketch a picture of the boys trying to break the bundle of sticks while the father watches.

The Story Sketcher might sketch a picture of the boys breaking the sticks one by one with the father watching.

The Story Sketcher might sketch a picture of the boys quarreling.

POSSIBLE EXPLANATIONS

The picture represents the main idea of the story.

The picture represents a humorous or unusual part of the story.

The picture represents a memorable part of the story.

The picture represents a part of the story that makes the reader happy, sad, frightened, etc.

The picture represents a clue to what will happen in the future or to what has happened in the past.

The picture represents something important to one of the characters.

The Daily Schedule

Lit Circles can be conducted successfully in forty-five minutes to an hour, three to five days per week. Each day students meet in their assigned groups and read seven to ten pages of their book, depending upon the chosen book. The teacher may decide how many pages at first. As students become more independent, you might want to let the group decide. Additional reading may be assigned as homework.

Typical Lit-Circle Session

Mini-Lesson, Pre-Reading and/or Vocabulary Activity	3 to 20 minutes
Reading	15 to 20 minutes
Lit-Log Entries	5 to 7 minutes
Role Preparation	3 to 5 minutes
Discussion and Role Presentation	7 to 10 minutes
Whole-Class Debriefing	5 to 10 minutes

Step-by-Step Directions

Pre-Reading, Mini-Lesson and/or Vocabulary Activity (3 to 20 minutes)

A mini-lesson may be any skill that the teacher decides is appropriate. It may focus on a word-attack skill, a critical-reading skill, a group-management skill, or an organizational skill. It may also be a vocabulary activity. You may want to ask students to complete the vocabulary activity independently before starting the reading. Another option is to have the activity done in pairs or as a group.

Reading (15 to 20 Minutes)

Instruct students to make notes of interesting words, phrases, and expressions, as they read. Also encourage them to note questions and observations that they want to discuss later with the group. They may include this information in their Lit Logs and/or by marking sections of the text with sticky notes. Students who finish ahead of time can work on a project or activity related to the reading. NOTE: Time for reading should be included in the session; however, there may be times when you feel it is better to assign all or some of the reading as homework.

Lit Log (5 to 7 Minutes)

This can be done in class or it can be done as a homework assignment depending upon where the reading was done. See the list of suggestions for responding in the Lit Log.

Role Preparation (3 to 5 Minutes)

This can be done in class or it can be done as a homework assignment depending upon where the reading was done.

Discussion (7 to 10 Minutes)

If students are not already in their small groups, they should gather at this time to discuss the portion of the book they have just read. Each student assumes the appropriate role at this time: Discussion Leader, Passage Perfecter, Vocabulary Detective, Creative Connector, Character Coordinator, Story Sketcher, and any you may have added. The Discussion Leader will use his or her questions or those created by the teacher to start the discussion. Open-ended questions and follow-up questions are the basis of the discussion. The group leader must make a real effort to be sure that everyone in the group participates in the discussion. Students may refer to notes made on sticky notes or in their Lit Logs to add points of interest to the discussion. The other students take turns performing their roles.

Debriefing (5 to 10 Minutes)

Following the reading and associated activities, a debriefing takes place with the entire class. During this time, problems and issues are discussed. The teacher may ask leading questions regarding literary techniques, behavior, connections to other classroom subjects, personal experiences, and so on. Debriefing also allows students to share comments about the story with their classmates. If a book being discussed has not been introduced in a Meet-the-Books session, the story should be summarized and enough information presented so that members of the other groups have basic knowledge about the book.

Mini-Lessons

Mini-lessons may be incorporated into a Lit-Circle reading period. These mini-lessons may vary in many ways. They may be only three or four minutes in length, or they may be as long as twenty minutes, depending upon the focus of the activity. Mini-lessons may precede the Lit-Circle session or they may be taught after it ends. Sometimes you will want to present the lesson to the entire class; other times you will want to aim your lesson at a particular group.

Skills and techniques that you might want to introduce or review in a mini-lesson include critical-reading skills, such as recognizing main ideas and details, inferencing, predicting, recognizing cause-and-effect relationships, recognizing fact and opinion, and comparing and contrasting; literary devices, such as imagery, flashback, and figurative language; grammar and writing conventions; vocabulary development; and creative-thinking skills. These mini-lessons should be relevant to the reading. For example, if there is flashback in the story, such as in *Where the Red Fern Grows,* it is appropriate to teach a mini-lesson on flashback.

Mini-Lesson Topics

The following are some of the skills that should be considered for Mini-Lessons.

Critical-Reading Skills

Compare and Contrast

Comprehension

Analysis

Predicting

Evaluation

Inference

Cause and Effect

Fact or Opinion

Main Idea and Detail

Interpretation

Sequence

Fiction or Non-fiction

Summarizing

Literary Skills

Figurative Language

Character Development

Plot

Setting

Conflict

Flashback

Mood

Dialogue

Theme

Imagery

Point of View

Symbolism

Irony

Grammar & Writing

Syntax

Sentence Structure & Variety

Punctuation

Capitalization

Parts of Speech

Creative-Thinking Skills

Synthesizing

Problem Solving

Decision Making

Creative Dramatics

Questioning Techniques

Vocabulary Building & Word Skills

Word-Attack Skills

Multiple Meanings

Application

Synonyms and Antonyms

Word Games

Analogies

Definitions

Structural Analysis

Mini-Lesson Samples

*The following mini-lessons are specific to works of popular children's literature.

Mini-Lesson #1: *Julie of the Wolves,* by Jean Craighead George
Spotlight Literary Skill
Point of View

Point of view is the voice that is used to tell the story plot. Some stories have a first-person narrator. A **first-person narrator** is the character who tells the story. That character refers to himself or herself as I and takes part in the story. In *Julie of the Wolves* the first-person narrator is Miyax.

Sometimes a story event can change when told from a different point of view. Describe these events from the different points of view as listed.

1. **The death of Miyax's mother**
   Miyax's point of view:_____
   Aunt Martha's point of view:_____

2. **Julie's marriage to Daniel**
   Aunt Martha's point of view:_____
   Naka's point of view:_____

3. **Julie's disappearance**
   Daniel's point of view:_____
   Pearl's point of view:_____

4. **The death of Amaroq**
   Aunt Martha's point of view:_____
   Pearl's point of view:_____

5. **Julie having a pen pal in San Francisco**
   Aunt Martha's point of view:_____
   Pearl's point of view:_____

Mini-Lesson #2: *A Year Down Yonder,* by Richard Peck
Spotlight Literary Skill
Conflict

Characters in stories must deal with different problems or struggles. Many times this act of struggling is what makes the story interesting. In *A Year Down Yonder* find…

1. **Character versus Character:** A character has a conflict with one or more other characters.
2 **Character versus Self:** A character must deal with a problem (physical or emotional) within him or herself.
3. **Character versus Society:** A character must deal with a part of society that is a problem for him or her (family, friends, community, government, rules, etc.).
4. **Character versus Nature:** A character must deal with a problem created by a natural force.

*The activities in this section were taken from the L-I-T *Guide*™ Series, written by the authors and published by Educational Impressions, Inc.

Mini-Lesson #3: *Maniac Magee,* by Jerry Spinelli
Spotlight Literary Skill
Compare and Contrast

In your readings you will often notice similarities and differences among characters, settings, and events. When you are asked to **compare things**, you must analyze the ways in which those things appear to be the same. When you are asked to **contrast** things, you must consider the ways in which those things appear to be different.

Compare and contrast the following characters and places from *Maniac Magee*. Then create Venn diagrams of your results.

Mars Bar and John McNab

East End and West End

Earl Grayson and Mrs. Beale

Mini-Lesson #4: *Holes,* by Louis Sachar
Spotlight Literary Skill
Flashback

Flashback is a literary technique in which the author interrupts the sequence of events to describe events that happened earlier. In *Holes*, Stanley experiences things in the present. The author frequently switches back in time, bringing in a character from the past. Of course, these characters from the past have an importance in the present.

Pretend that you are interviewing the grown-up Stanley Yelnats IV. What questions would you ask about his life since the story ended? Write a list of five questions. Then exchange with a classmate to create possible answers for each.

Now use an example from the story to illustrate flashback. Explain how the flashback is important to the story of the grown-up Stanley.

Mini-Lesson #5: *Johnny Tremain,* by Esther Forbes
Spotlight Literary Skill
Historical Fiction

Historical fiction is a type of writing in which true facts are mixed with fiction. These imaginative stories often include real names, dates, and historical settings to make the tale seem more true to life. *Johnny Tremain* is an example of historical fiction.

In this activity you are asked to separate the fact from the fiction found in this story. On the left, make a list of historically true facts. On the right, make a list of fictional occurrences in the story. An example of each is given to you.

HISTORICAL FACTS	FICTIONAL FACTS
John Hancock and Samuel Adams were leaders of the American Revolution.	Johnny was burned making a silver sugar basin.

Mini-Lesson #6: *Bridge to Terabithia,* by Katherine Paterson
Spotlight Literary Skill
Figurative Language

The use of figurative language helps to enrich all types of writing. Katherine Paterson uses various types of figurative language to create mental pictures that make the dialogue and descriptions more vivid.

A **simile** is a stated comparison between two dissimilar things. The word "like" or "as" is used to make the comparison. EXAMPLE: "Mama would be mad as flies in a fruit jar."

A **metaphor** is a stated comparison between two dissimilar things without the use of "like" or "as." EXAMPLE: "But it was she who was the diamond, sparkling out of that muddy…setting."

Personification is the bestowing of human characteristics upon lifeless objects or abstract ideas. EXAMPLE: "The dogwood and redbud played hide and seek between the oaks and evergreens."

Look for figures of speech in *Bridge to Terabithia* and write them in the chart. For each, identify the type of figure of speech being used and then explain what dissimilar things are being compared or what is being personified. Note the page where each is found.

FIGURES OF SPEECH

Excerpt	*Figure of Speech*	*Explanation*

Mini-Lesson #7: *Out of the Dust,* by Karen Hesse
Spotlight Literary Skill
Theme

Theme is a central idea in a story. It should not be confused with the series of events, or plot, of a story. One important theme of *Out of the Dust* is the idea of courage in the face of adversity. Another theme brought out by the author is the idea of forgiveness. A third theme might be dealing with a physical limitation.

Part 1: Find examples of each theme in the story.

_____
_____
_____
_____
_____

Part 2: Share a personal experience relating to each theme.

_____
_____
_____
_____
_____
_____
_____
_____

Lit-Log Suggestions

The following list represents ways in which you can respond to what you have read. You will want to record these in your Lit Log for easy reference.

1. Write your answers to the comprehension and discussion questions. Be sure to include reasons for your responses. Note any page numbers that you might want to refer to during discussion periods.

2. Use your Lit Log to record vocabulary activities that have been assigned. Also record definitions of other unfamiliar or unusual words.

3. Jot down comments about plot development. How is it developing? Have you been able to follow it easily? Is any of the story confusing?

4. Describe a personal connection to what you have read? How does something in the story relate to you? How does it make you feel?

5. Make predictions about what you think will happen in the chapters that follow.

6. Record any examples of figurative or colorful language. You might note similes, metaphors, personifications, slang, hyperbole, colloquialisms, and other interesting language.

7. Compare and contrast events, characters, and language within the story to each other and to those in other stories you have read. Remember, to *compare* you focus on likenesses and to *contrast* you focus on differences. (Sometimes "compare" is used to refer to both likenesses and differences.)

8. Look for examples of character development in the day's reading. The author paints a picture of the characters by telling us what they say, how they act, what they think, and what others say about them.

9. Describe the main setting of the story and any other important settings. You may even want to make a sketch of the setting.

10. Record any questions you may have about a confusing part. The following are examples of what you might write.

    I don't understand why _____ did _____.

    I don't know why _____ wanted to _____.

    Does _____ mean that _____?

11. Make a connection to something else you have read by the same author or on the same topic or theme. Was there something discussed in class to which you can connect the story?

12. Give some examples of interesting dialogue. Be sure to note the page and paragraph for easy reference. Explain why you find the particular dialogue interesting.

13. Do you know more information about something mentioned in the story? Make a note to discuss this with your group or with the entire class.

14. Make a note about something you find interesting. Look for more information about this topic. Use the internet, the encyclopedia, or reference books.

15. After finishing the story, write a review of the book. Include the not-so-good points as well as the good ones. Discuss the vocabulary and readability for your grade level. Was it too easy? Was it too difficult? Mention why you believe others would or would not enjoy the book.

16. Use your Lit Log to record ideas for your post-reading activities.

Lit-Log Entry

Student's Name: _____

Book: _____

Pages Read: _____   Date: _____

RESPONSES TO DISCUSSION QUESTIONS

Question:

_____

_____

_____

Response:

_____

_____

_____

_____

_____

_____

Comments:

_____

_____

_____

VOCABULARY

_____

_____

_____

_____

_____

EXAMPLES OF FIGURATIVE LANGUAGE

_____

_____

_____

CHARACTER AND PLOT DEVELOPMENT

_____

_____

_____

_____

PERSONAL CONNECTIONS, CONFUSING PARTS, AND OTHER THOUGHTS

_____

_____

_____

_____

Sample Response to a Discussion Question for *A Single Shard*

LIT-LOG ENTRY

Student's Name: <u>Tania B.</u>

Book and Author: <u>A Single Shard, by Linda Sue Park</u>

Pages Read: <u>82 to 89</u>   Date: <u>October 30</u>

RESPONSES TO DISCUSSION QUESTIONS

Question: Do you think Tree-ear was responsible for the loss of the vases?

Response:

I don't think that Tree-ear should feel responsible for losing the vases. He fought very hard to protect them. He was up against two men who had a lot of experience robbing people. I think they picked on him because he was just a boy. They thought it would be easy to rob him.

Comments:

I think that Tree-ear should be proud of how hard he fought against the robbers. Maybe I would have given up more easily than he did.

Questioning Techniques

Questions used in Lit Circles should require explanation, interpretation, and connections. They should helps students understand what was read, enhance the enjoyment of the literature, and elicit discussion. Students respond to issues, literary devices, and characters. When answering questions, students must provide examples from the story to support their responses. From time to time you may wish to ask students to expand their answers to a comprehension or discussion question into an essay. This may be done in their Lit Log.

Model for and with your students the skill of asking questions whose answers require complete sentences with supporting information. Pose your questions in such a way that they promote discussion without dominating it. Follow-up questions, which encourage students to examine the questions more thoroughly, should be encouraged. Differences of opinion should be expected.

Comparison of Methods

Traditional Method

A question is asked.

A question is answered.

A new question is asked.

Lit-Circles Method

A question is asked.

A question is answered.

Other answers are elicited.

Follow-up questions are asked.

Examples from the text are used to support responses.

Bloom's Taxonomy

Creating questions that elicit higher-level thinking requires practice. Benjamin Bloom described six levels of cognitive thinking. From lowest to highest the levels are knowledge, comprehension, application, analysis, synthesis, and evaluation. Certain verbs tend to elicit each level of thinking. When creating questions, it is helpful to keep these verbs in mind.

Thinking Skill	Verbs That Correspond	
KNOWLEDGE Knowledge is the recalling of information, bringing to mind the appropriate material.	Tell Describe Locate Find Name	List Retell Write State
COMPREHENSION Comprehension is the understanding of the information being communicated.	Comprehend Explain Rewrite Define	Paraphrase Interpret Restate
APPLICATION Application is using, or applying, the information in a new situation.	Solve Use Illustrate Examine Construct	Show Calculate Complete Classify
ANALYSIS Analysis is separating information into its component parts.	Analyze Distinguish Examine Compare Contrast	Investigate Categorize Identify Separate Advertise
SYNTHESIS Synthesis is creating a "whole" from the parts, building upon what is known.	Create Invent Compose Improve Propose Plan	Construct Design Imagine Formulate Devise Predict
EVALUATION Evaluation is making value judgments based upon established criteria.	Judge Select Choose Decide Discuss Justify Assess	Debate Verify Argue Recommend Determine Prioritize Rate

Creating Good Questions
USING BLOOM'S TAXONOMY

When taking part in a Lit-Circle discussion, it is important to ask questions that call for higher-level thinking—application and above. Use the Bloom's Taxonomy Chart to help you create sample questions for the indicated level of thinking. Your questions may relate to literature or to any other area of the curriculum. Circle the verb that corresponds to the level.

KNOWLEDGE

1. _____

2. _____

COMPREHENSION

1. _____

2. _____

APPLICATION

1. _____

2. _____

3. _____

ANALYSIS

1. _____

2. _____

3. _____

SYNTHESIS

1. _____

2. _____

3. _____

EVALUATION

1. _____

2. _____

3. _____

Open-Ended Questions
GENERAL PROMPTS

You should strive for open-ended questions. Avoid questions that can be answered with a simple "yes" or "no." Brainstorm with your students to create a list of open-ended questions that can be used for many works of literature. (In this section the term "question" refers to any expression of inquiry that calls for a reply. It may or may not be an interrogative sentence.)

Open-Ended Questions to Be Used with Many Books:

1.   Explain in your own words…

2.   What do you think happened after ___?

3.   Can you distinguish between ___ and ___?

4.   If you could ask ___ a question, what would you ask?

5.   In what ways can you identify with ___?

6.   What part of this story could really have happened?

7.   What part of this story could not really have happened?

8.   If ___ happened, what effect would that have on ___?

9.   What were some of the reasons for ___ behaving ___?

10. How is ___ like (different from) ___?

11. In what ways did ___ change from the beginning of the story? What caused the change?

12. What was ___ 's solution to the problem? Evaluate that solution.

13. How would you have handled the situation?

14. Justify ___'s actions.

15. Explain what ___ meant when (s)he said, "___."

16. What do you think of the way that ___?

17. Why, do you think, did ___ ___?

18. Compare and contrast ___ and ___.

19. How does the author show you the personality of this character?

20. What caused ___ to say ___?

Open-Ended Questions
SPECIFIC PROMPTS

*The following open-ended questions are specific to works of popular children's literature.

The Great Gilly Hopkins, by Katherine Paterson
If you could have a conversation with Gilly Hopkins, what would you say?

The House of Dies Drear, by Virginia Hamilton
Compare and contrast Mayhew's and Pluto's views of the treasures of Dies Drear. Why, do you think, did Pluto seem comfortable about having Mr. Small learn the secret of the cave?

Roll of Thunder, Hear My Cry, by Mildred Taylor
The author stated that she created the Logan family in order to provide the African-American heroes that were missing from the schoolbooks that she had read as a child. How has she made the characters seem heroic? Write at least one example of a character's courageous behavior.

A Day No Pigs Would Die, by Richard Peck
Explain Rob's remark: "Fences sure are funny, aren't they Papa."

The Whipping Boy, by Sid Fleishman
In Chapter 15 Jemmy had an opportunity to separate himself from Prince Brat…At the last second, Jemmy shouted, "Stop. Cap'n!…We left me friend behind." Put yourself in Jemmy's place. What would you have done? Why?

Holes, by Louis Sachar
Judge Stanley's decision to take the truck to find Zero.

My Brother Sam Is Dead, by James Lincoln Collier and Christopher Collier
Tim used a simile in describing his hunger. Compose an original simile or metaphor that describes how you feel when you are hungry, tired, or scared.

The Midwife's Apprentice, by Karen Cushman
In what way did the midwife's evaluation of Alyce differ from Alyce's opinion of herself?

Bud, Not Buddy, by Christopher Paul Curtis
What type of racism did the band encounter on their road trips? How did Herman E. Calloway deal with the problem? In your opinion, would this situation occur in today's world? Why or why not?

Crispin: The Cross of Lead, by Avi
Bear says, "Both wheat and trust take a full season to grow." Do you agree? Have you ever trusted someone too soon—before you knew him or her well enough?

*The questions in this section were taken from the L-I-T *Guide*™ Series, written by the authors and published by Educational Impressions, Inc.

Pick a Project
GENERAL

Projects that require critical or creative thinking greatly enhance the students' understanding and retention of the story. This section makes it easier for students to select and create a meaningful extension project. Students may work on the projects individually or in small groups.

The following project ideas may be cut into slips, mounted on cardboard or oak tag, and placed in a classroom container for students to consider. A Project Planning Sheet is included to help students formulate their project ideas. Also provided are examples of Post-Reading Activities from several L-I-T *Guides*™.

Projects

- -

BOARD GAME

Create a board game based on the events and characters in your book. Include clear directions for play. Have a class game day and share the games that you and your classmates have designed.

- -

STORY MAP

Design a story map. Show places and events that are important to the plot of the story. Label each.

- -

AWARD

Create an award. Tell which story character should receive it. Write a speech telling why the character deserves the award. Present the speech to your classmates.

- -

DICTIONARY

Compile a class dictionary of new and unusual words that you have read in the story. Give each classmate a copy.

- -

More Projects

- -

NEWS STORY

Write a news story that summarizes the story events and describes the main characters' accomplishments. Create a headline for your story.

- -

POSTER

Design a colorful poster that will encourage others to read the book that you have just completed. Include important information, such as the author's name and a highlight of the book. Place the poster in the hallway or the library of your school.

- -

INTERVIEW

Suppose you had the opportunity to interview the main character. Think of five questions that you would ask the character. Write down the questions and the answers that the character would give.

- -

PROBLEM SOLVING

The main character of the book encounters many problems. Choose one of the problems and tell how you would have solved it differently. Be sure to explain your reasoning.

- -

More Projects

- -

PUPPET SHOW

Create a puppet show based on the story. With your cooperative-learning group, write a script and make puppets representing the story characters. Perform your puppet show for your classmates.

- -

IT PAYS TO ADVERTISE!

Design an advertising campaign for the book you have just read. Plan your campaign for different media, such as TV, radio, magazine, or billboard. Emphasize reasons for people to buy or read the book.

- -

ROLLER CINEMA

Create a roller cinema to show important scenes from the book. Draw the scenes on white construction paper and tape them together. Then tape each end to a dowel. Make 2 holes and a screen in the box. Put the dowels in the holes. Turn the dowels to roll the pictures.

- -

PATCHWORK QUILT

Select favorite or main events from your book and illustrate them on pre-cut paper squares. Glue the completed squares onto a colorful backdrop to make a "Story Patchwork Quilt."

- -

More Projects

- -

COMIC STRIP

Create a comic strip or comic book based on the characters and events in the story. Write the dialogue in "word bubbles."

- -

MOBILE

Use construction paper, string, and a wire hanger to create a mobile. Attach pictures of characters, settings, or events to the wire hanger. Label the pictures. Make sure there is a picture or writing on both sides of the paper.

- -

POEM

Write a poem that reflects your thoughts and feelings about the story. Use figurative language such as similes, metaphors, hyperbole, and personification to make your poetry more colorful.

- -

SCRAPBOOK

Make a scrapbook that includes "photos" of characters, souvenirs of events, or items that are featured in the story. Be creative!

- -

More Projects

- -

PANEL DISCUSSION

Select students to be part of a classroom panel discussion on the main theme of the book or a controversial issue in the story.

- -

COLLAGE

Make a character collage to represent the traits, appearance, interests, and personality of one of the main characters in the story you just read. Use magazine cutouts and a variety of other materials to make your collage interesting.

- -

COMPARE AND CONTRAST

Compare and contrast a character or characters in this story to characters in other stories that you have read. Construct a chart to record your findings.

- -

EPILOGUE

An epilogue is a short concluding section at the end of a novel. It often tells about the future of the characters. Write an epilogue for the story you have just completed.

- -

More Projects

- -

DIARY

Imagine that you are one of the main characters in the story. Write a diary of your daily thoughts, hopes, and fears. Also record your impressions of other characters in the story.

- -

CHARACTER MAP

Choose a memorable story character. Sketch a picture of the character in the center of a large sheet of paper. Think of ways that you could describe that character: actions, dialogue, traits, physical description, etc. Write these descriptive words and phrases around the picture. Use a different script or computer font to make the paper attractive.

- -

MURAL

Along with a group of classmates, create a mural to represent the important highlights of the story and main characters. Upon completion, display it on a classroom bulletin board or wall.

- -

LETTER WRITING

Write a letter to your favorite character. Tell what you admired about him or her. Explain what you might have done differently to solve a problem or give the character advice about a problem.

- -

Project Planning Sheet

NAME: _____

TITLE OF BOOK: _____

TYPE OF PROJECT: _____

DATE DUE: _____

RESEARCH NEEDED

_____

_____

_____

MATERIALS NEEDED

_____

_____

Explain why you chose this project. How does it reflect a theme or character(s) in the story.

_____

_____

_____

_____

How will you present your project to your teacher and classmates?

_____

_____

_____

_____

What other audiences might be interested in sharing your project information?

_____

_____

_____

Post-Reading Activities
SPECIFIC

*The following post-reading activities are specific to works of popular children's literature.

Island of the Blue Dolphins, by Scott O'Dell
Create a map of the Island of the Blue Dolphins showing the following places mentioned in the story: Black Cave, Tall Rock, Sea Elephant, the ravine, the cliff, and Coral Cave. Where do you think these places were located? Use the book as a reference and be prepared to back up your choices with reasons.

A Single Shard, by Linda Sue Park
In your classroom or art class, use clay to replicate an item of pottery described in the story. Some examples are the monkey, the box, the melon-shaped vase, and the thousand-crane vase. Create a display of the work created by you and your classmates in a classroom "art museum."

Charlotte's Web, by E. B. White
Pretend that you are Wilbur and write a **eulogy** for your friend. A eulogy is a speech or writing in praise of someone, usually someone who has died. Try to recall story events that show Wilbur's love for his friend Charlotte. Work with other students in a cooperative-learning group to develop a eulogy in Charlotte's honor. Compare your completed project with those of others in your class.

Out of the Dust, by Karen Hesse
You are there. Imagine that it is 1935 in Oklahoma and that you are a reporter at the scene of a destructive dust storm. Use your senses to describe what is happening as the wind whips by you. Tell what you see, hear, and feel.

The Outsiders, by S. E. Hinton
A **stereotype** is a character with exaggerated personality traits who falsely represents a group of people. Read the list of characters and think of one or more character traits that make the character seem stereotyped: Dallas, Ponyboy, Two-Bit, Cherry, Randy, and Johnny.

Johnny Tremain, by Esther Forbes
Conduct a mock trial in the classroom. Simulate the trial in which Johnny is accused of stealing from Merchant Lyte. Assign the following roles: Merchant Lyte, the lawyers, the judge, Cilia, Johnny, Isannah and other witnesses, and a jury.

The Door in the Wall, by Marguerite de Angeli
Research the architecture of a medieval castle. Learn architectural terms such as bailey, turret, portcullis, and keep. Use the research to plan your own "dream castle."

*The activities in this section were taken from the L-I-T *Guide*™ Series, written by the authors and published by Educational Impressions, Inc.

© Educational Impressions, Inc.

More Post-Reading Activities
SPECIFIC

Harry Potter and the Sorcerer's Stone, by J. K. Rowling
In Chapter 17 Dumbledore made several meaningful statements. Write a paragraph with one of the following statements as the main idea:

"Fear of a name increases fear of the thing itself."

"To have been loved so deeply, even though the person who loved you is gone, will give us protection forever."

"It takes a great deal of bravery to stand up to our enemies, but just as much to stand up to our friends."

Shiloh, by Phyllis Reynolds Naylor
Point of view is the voice used to tell the story plot. In *Shiloh* the storyteller is Marty. Summarize the story first from Shiloh's point of view and then from the point of view of Judd Travers.

A Year Down Yonder, by Richard Peck
Learn what causes tornadoes and why they are so prevalent in the midwestern part of the United States. Make a poster of your findings. Report to the class on safety procedures to take if a tornado is predicted.

Julie of the Wolves, by Jean Craighead George
Although Miyax was looking forward to giving up her family traditions and moving to San Francisco with Amy, she later realized that her heritage was very important to her. List some customs and traditions of your own heritage. Bring to class some objects or foods that reflect that culture to share with others.

From the Mixed-up Files of Mrs. Basil E. Frankweiler, by E. L. Konigsburg
Although everything turned out well for Claudia and Jamie, the act of running away from home can be a perilous adventure. With your classmates, discuss the real-life problems and dangers associated with running away from home.

A Wrinkle in Time, by Madeleine L'Engle
In *A Wrinkle in Time,* Meg, Charles Wallace, and Calvin travel through time to Camazotz, a strange city ruled by an evil power. In this activity, you are asked to use your imagination to create your own city of the future. Write and/or sketch your ideas for each category. Then sketch a detailed city plan on a larger sheet of paper. You may wish to combine all of your ideas into a booklet. Include the following: Name of City, Government and Laws, Industries, Education, Sports, Public and Private Transportation, Architecture, and Monetary System.

Story Skit
DIRECTIONS

Creating a story script and performing it before an audience is a wonderful culminating experience for your students and an excellent way to reinforce comprehension. Here are some tips for creating a successful story skit.

- Have each Lit-Circle group choose a story or a special part of a story to dramatize.

- Encourage students to re-read the story before preparing the script.

- Encourage students to select a story that has adequate dialogue.

- Assign character and narrator roles or ask students to select the roles they wish to portray.

- Assign one member of each Lit Circle to be the scriptwriter and to record the group members' ideas. This role should change at each writing session.

- Instruct the whole class on how to use a play format to retell the story. Model an example of script dialogue on the chalkboard or overhead projector. Show them how to use the character's name followed by a colon. Explain that stage directions are words that provide instructions to the actors on how to move on stage and how to recite their dialogue. Stage directions always appear in parentheses.

    EXAMPLE
    Samantha: (In a nervous voice) I think I heard something move near the bushes. Could it be a bear?

    Alex: (Opens the flap of the tent) Don't worry. It's probably just the park ranger checking the area.

- Send an invitation to classmates, family, and friends to attend the performance. (A sample is provided on the next page.)

Story Skit
INVITATION

Dear _____,

      Our Lit-Circle group has been reading
_____.
As a culminating activity, we have turned the book into a play. We would be very happy if you could attend the performance.

Date

_____

Time

_____

Place

_____

      We hope that you will share this special day with us!

Love,

_____

Story Skit
WORKSHEET

Each member of the group should have a copy of this worksheet to organize ideas for the story skit. All members should contribute ideas. Remember to develop your skit in logical order. If the skit is long, divide it into acts and scenes. Choose one group member to be the recorder.

LIT-CIRCLE MEMBERS

_____   _____

_____   _____

_____   _____

BOOK ON WHICH SKIT IS BASED

TITLE: _____

AUTHOR: _____

CHARACTERS	**PORTRAYED BY...**
_____	_____
_____	_____
_____	_____

NARRATOR: _____

PROPS AND OTHER NECESSARY ITEMS

_____   _____

_____   _____

_____   _____

_____   _____

Story Skit
WRITING THE SCRIPT

Write the rough draft of your skit on this page. Remember to give stage directions so that actors know where and how to move.

_____

_____

_____

_____

_____

_____

_____

_____

_____

_____

_____

_____

_____

_____

_____

_____

_____

_____

_____

_____

Literary Wax Museum
INTRODUCTION

A Literary "Wax" Museum is a unique and enjoyable activity in which students have an opportunity to display their understanding of the characters in a story in a creative way. Set a time, date, and place for the event. Create a schedule for each student, making sure that no student is required to stand for more than ten to fifteen minutes, depending on the age of the students.

Literary Wax Museum
STUDENT DIRECTIONS

A Literary "Wax" Museum provides an opportunity for you to display your understanding of the characters in the book you have just read in a creative way. You will be asked to be a "wax figure" of a character of the book you have just read. As such you will be required to stand for a short period of time. You will also be required to supply information about the character. This information will be read by another student. You, in turn, may be asked to read information written by one of your classmates.

- Choose a character from the book you have just read.

- Think about how your "wax figure" should look. How can you dress up to look like the character you have selected? What props will you need? Keep in mind the following: physical appearance, clothing, habits, hobbies, favorite foods, favorite games, pets, etc. Remember, sometimes just a hat, scarf, vest, stuffed animal, or other item can be added to identify a character.

- Sketch your ideas on paper. When you are satisfied with your sketch, gather the clothing and props you will need. Try them on to see if they have the desired effect.

- Decide on the character information you will provide for your docent, or museum guide, to read. Write about the character's physical appearance, character traits, problems he or she must overcome, the manner in which he or she solves problems, how the character relates to other characters in the story, and why this character is outstanding.

- Use the information you have compiled about the character to create a presentation for the Wax Museum. Write the information on a card. This card will be read by one of your classmates, who will play the role of docent, or museum guide, while you are posing as the story character.

- Read your presentation. See how long it takes to read it aloud. Be sure that it is not longer than the time your teacher has allotted for each "wax figure" to stand.

- Create an invitation to invite family and friends to the event. (A sample is provided.)

Literary Wax Museum
WORKSHEET

TITLE OF BOOK: _____

AUTHOR: _____

CHARACTER: _____

DESCRIPTION OF CHARACTER:

_____

_____

_____

_____

PROPS AND OTHER NECESSARY ITEMS

_____   _____

_____   _____

_____   _____

_____   _____

INFORMATION FOR DOCENT:

_____

_____

_____

_____

_____

_____

_____

_____

_____

_____

Literary Wax Museum
SKETCH OF WAX FIGURE

Literary Wax Museum
INVITATION

Dear _____,

    Our Lit-Circle group has been reading
_____.
As a culminating activity, we have planned a "Wax Museum" presentation. The name of the character I will portray is _____.

Date

_____

Time

_____

Place

_____

    We hope that you will share this special day with us!

Love,

_____

Lit Bowl
VARIATIONS

A fun and interesting way to complete a marking period or a semester of reading is to conduct a literature bowl. There are many variations of this type of competition. Three are described below. Use one of them or your own version.

VARIATION ONE
A Lit Bowl may be conducted as an oral contest. In this form, the captain answers for the team after conferring with team members for the answers.

VARIATION TWO
A Lit Bowl may be conducted as a written exercise in which each team member writes the answer independently. The teacher checks responses, tallies the individual scores, and averages them for a team score.

VARIATION THREE
A Lit Bowl may be conducted in the same manner as a spelling bee. If this format is chosen, begin with the easiest questions and progress to the most difficult.

Most students love Lit Bowls! Don't be surprised if it spreads to other classes. It may even become a schoolwide competition!

Lit Bowl
SUGGESTIONS

Keep the following in mind when preparing for and conducting a Lit Bowl.

WORKS TO INCLUDE
Base your questions on all of the stories read in class during the marking period, semester, or year. Include stories read to the class by you, those read by the entire class, and those read during Lit Circles and shared with the entire class.

CATEGORIES
Suggested categories for questions include authors, titles, characters, themes, settings, and problems encountered. Other related categories are literary devices and figurative-language terms. You may also combine categories.

POINTS
Assign a point value to the questions based on their level of difficulty. You may want to differentiate them by putting them on color-coded index cards or colored paper. With each turn, the individual or team requests the point value of the question to attempt. Note: The points assigned to a question will depend in part upon the emphasis placed on the information during class discussions and lessons.

RULES
Decide upon the rules concerning incorrect answers, disruptive behavior, and how the winner is determined before the Lit Bowl begins. You should discuss these rules with the students and elicit their input.

FORMATION OF TEAMS
Decide how you will group the children and which format you will use. If you decide that they will work in teams, choose a captain for each and decide on the responsibilities the captain will have. Each team should comprise students from different Lit-Circle groups. If possible, have at least one student who has read each book on each team. Ideally, through the Meet-the Book sessions, whole-class debriefings, and teacher read-alouds, all of the students will have been exposed to the main pieces of information regarding most of the books upon which the questions will be based.

Lit Bowl
SAMPLE QUESTIONS

The following are examples of questions that might be asked during a Lit-Bowl competition. Of course, the difficulty depends upon the grade level and reading level of the students. Use your discretion in assigning point values to the questions you include. Keep in mind the emphasis previously placed on the various aspects of the books during classroom lessons and discussions.

Write the point value on each card. You may want to write or print the questions on sheets of colored index cards or other paper. Each color would represent a different value. In this way there is less chance of a mix-up if the cards inadvertently are placed in the wrong pile. **With each turn, the individual or team may request the point value of the question to be answered.**

SAMPLE TEN-POINT QUESTIONS

1. Who is the author of *Peter Rabbit?*

2. Name one of the main characters in *Charlotte's Web.*

3. Name the author of *The Ugly Duckling.*

4. What is the name of the school attended by Harry Potter?

5. What is the setting of *Island of the Blue Dolphins?*

SAMPLE TWENTY-FIVE-POINT QUESTIONS

1. Which Lois Lowry story is set in Denmark during World War II?

2. In what novel does Stanley Yelnats appear?

3. In which book does Miyax leave her home in Alaska and walk to San Francisco?

4. Name two books by Gary Paulsen.

5. Name Marguerite de Angeli's novel about a boy named Robin who lives in medieval England.

SAMPLE FIFTY-POINT QUESTIONS

1. *Johnny Tremain, Across Five Aprils,* and *My Brother Sam Is Dead* are set during times of war. Give the correct war period for each novel.

2. In *Witch of Blackbird Pond,* Kit moves to New England from her island home. Name the island.

3. Name a book by Beverly Cleary in which the story is told through letter writing.

4. In *Crispin: The Cross of Lead,* Crispin and his companion share a dangerous adventure. Name the companion.

5. Name two important characters in *A Single Shard.*

REMARKABLE READER

This certificate is awarded to

_____

in recognition of being the

LIT-BOWL CHAMPION

OF _____.

Presented this _____ day of _____, 20___

by _____.

General Planning Sheet

Teacher: _____

Grade Level: _____

Number of Students in Class: _____

Number of Groups in Class: _____

GROUP 1 MEMBERS

_____

_____

_____

_____

GROUP 2 MEMBERS

_____

_____

_____

_____

GROUP 3 MEMBERS

_____

_____

_____

_____

GROUP 4 MEMBERS

_____

_____

_____

_____

GROUP 5 MEMBERS

_____

_____

_____

_____

GROUP 6 MEMBERS

_____

_____

_____

_____

Specific Group Planning Sheet

Teacher: _____

Grade Level: _____   **Group Number:** _____

Title and Author of Book: _____

Starting Date: _____

SCHEDULE FOR CIRCLE DISCUSSIONS

_____   _____

_____   _____

_____   _____

_____   _____

TYPES OF MINI-LESSONS

_____   _____

_____   _____

_____   _____

TYPES OF ROLES

_____   _____

_____   _____

_____   _____

SPECIAL ASSIGNMENTS: _____

_____

SPECIAL CONCERNS: _____

_____

_____

Completion Date: _____

Teacher Observation Form

Use this form to help you evaluate the students when they are working in their Lit Circles. Judge the students' overall behavior and participation as you walk from group to group. Use this rating scale or design your own.

Student's Name: _____ **Date:** _____

Title of Book: _____

N = Not Observed   R = Rarely   S = Sometimes   U = Usually   A = Always

SOCIAL BEHAVIOR

Participates often   _____

Encourages others to participate   _____

Is prepared   _____

Offers personal connections   _____

Listens without interrupting   _____

Shares ideas and cooperates   _____

Values others' contributions   _____

Keeps the discussion flowing   _____

READING SKILLS

Makes inferences   _____

Makes predictions   _____

Compares and contrasts   _____

Uses passages from the book to support ideas   _____

Makes judgments with reason   _____

Analyzes characters   _____

Does reading and other assignments   _____

Keeps Lit Log up to date   _____

Rereads to understand details   _____

Understands cause and effect   _____

Understands author's purpose   _____

Is familiar with figurative language   _____

Asks meaningful questions relating to the story   _____

Understands story structure (plot, setting, conflict, resolution) _____

Teacher Record Form
INDIVIDUAL ASSESSMENT

Use this form to list grades for various assignments relating to the Lit Circle. Use one form for each Lit Circle.

Title of Book: _____

Student's Name	Lit-Log Grade	Project Grade	Book-Test Grade	Participation Grade
_____	_____	_____	_____	_____
_____	_____	_____	_____	_____
_____	_____	_____	_____	_____
_____	_____	_____	_____	_____
_____	_____	_____	_____	_____
_____	_____	_____	_____	_____
_____	_____	_____	_____	_____
_____	_____	_____	_____	_____
_____	_____	_____	_____	_____
_____	_____	_____	_____	_____
_____	_____	_____	_____	_____
_____	_____	_____	_____	_____
_____	_____	_____	_____	_____
_____	_____	_____	_____	_____
_____	_____	_____	_____	_____
_____	_____	_____	_____	_____
_____	_____	_____	_____	_____
_____	_____	_____	_____	_____

Group-Evaluation Form

Group and Book _____

Member's Name _____

Date: _____

1. Which best represents the way your group members cooperated?

    ALWAYS   MOST OF THE TIME   SOMETIMES   VERY LITTLE

2. What, do you think, were your group's strengths?

    _____

    _____

    _____

3. What, do you think, were your group's weaknesses?

    _____

    _____

    _____

4. Describe the ways in which you helped one another?

    _____

    _____

    _____

5. What did this group experience teach you?

    _____

    _____

6. Suggest ways in which the group could improve.

    _____

    _____

7. Rate your group from 1 to 10, with 10 being the best possible. Circle the number.

    1   2   3   4   5   6   7   8   9   10

Self-Evaluation Form

Group and Book _____

Member's Name _____

Date: _____

1. What Lit-Circle role or roles did you have while reading this book?

   _____

2. What did you like about the role(s)?

   _____

   _____

   _____

3. What did you dislike about the role(s)?

   _____

   _____

   _____

4. Rate your level of involvement and responsibility. Then explain your response.

          EXCELLENT   GOOD   FAIR   POOR

   COMMENTS: _____

   _____

5. Rate the level of difficulty of the book you just read. Then explain your response.

          TOO EASY   TOO HARD   JUST RIGHT

   COMMENTS: _____

   _____

6. Describe the assignment or activity that you enjoyed the most and give your reasons.

   _____

   _____

   _____

Reading Record

Use this form to compile a record of each student's reading habits to determine his or her range of topics. If the range is too narrow, you can suggest titles to broaden the student's reading interests. Along with literature-circle books, independent reading choices may also be included on the form.

Student's Name _____

TITLE OF BOOK	AUTHOR	DATE COMPLETED

Glossary

Alliteration: Repetition of initial (beginning) sounds in 2 or more consecutive or neighboring words.

Analogy: A comparison based upon the resemblance in some particular ways between things that are otherwise unlike.

Anecdote: A short account of an interesting, amusing, or biographical occurrence.

Anticlimax: An event that is less important than what occurred before it.

Archaic language: Language that was once common in a particular historic period but which is no longer commonly used.

Cause and effect: The relationship in which one condition brings about another condition as a direct result. The result, or consequence, is called the effect.

Character development: The ways in which the author shows how a character changes as the story proceeds.

Characterization: The method used by the author to give readers information about a character; a description or representation of a person's qualities or peculiarities.

Classify: To arrange according to a category or trait.

Climax: The moment when the action in a story reaches its greatest conflict.

Compare and contrast: To examine the likenesses and differences of two people, ideas, or things. (*Contrast* emphasizes differences. *Compare* may focus on likenesses alone or on likenesses and differences.)

Conflict: The main source of drama and tension in a literary work; the discord between persons or forces that brings about dramatic action.

Connotation: Something suggested or implied, not actually stated.

Description: An account that gives the reader a mental image or picture of something.

Dialect: A form of language used in a certain geographic region; it is distinguished from the standard form of the language by pronunciation, grammar, and/or vocabulary.

Dialogue (dialog): The parts of a literary work that represent conversation.

Fact: A piece of information that can be proven or verified.

Figurative language: Description of one thing in terms usually used for something else. Simile and metaphor are examples of figurative language.

Flashback: The insertion of an earlier event into the normal chronological sequence of a narrative.

Foreshadowing: The use of clues to give readers a hint of events that will occur later on.

Historical fiction: Fiction represented in a setting true to the history of the time in which the story takes place.

Imagery: Language that appeals to the senses; the use of figures of speech or vivid descriptions to produce mental images.

Irony: The use of words to express the opposite of their literal meaning.

Legend: A story handed down from earlier times; its truth is popularly accepted but can't be verified.

Limerick: Humorous 5-lined poem with form *aabba*. Lines 1, 2 and 5 are longer than lines 3 and 4.

Metaphor: A figure of speech that compares two unlike things without the use of "like" or "as."

Mood: The feeling that the author creates for the reader.

Motivation: The reasons for the behavior of a character.

Narrative: The type of writing that tells a story.

Narrator: The character who tells the story.

Opinion: A personal point of view or belief.

Parody: Writing that ridicules or imitates something more serious.

Personification: Figure of speech in which an inanimate object or an abstract idea is given human characteristics.

Play: A literary work written in dialogue form and usually performed before an audience.

Plot: The arrangement or sequence of events in a story.

Point of view: The perspective from which a story is told.

Protagonist: The main character.

Pun: A play on words that are similar in sound but different in meaning.

Realistic fiction: True-to-life fiction; people, places, and happenings are similar to those in real life.

Resolution: Part of the plot (from climax on) where the main dramatic conflict is worked out.

Satire: A literary work that pokes fun at individual or societal weaknesses.

Sequencing: The placement of story elements in the order of their occurrence.

Setting: The time and place in which the story occurs.

Simile: A figure of speech that uses "like" or "as" to compare two unlike things.

Stereotype: A character whose personality traits represent a group rather than an individual.

Suspense: Quality that causes readers to wonder what will happen next.

Symbolism: The use of a thing, character, object, or idea to represent something else.

Synonyms: Words that are very similar in meaning.

Tall tale: An exaggerated story detailing unbelievable events.

Theme: The main idea of a literary work; the message the author wants to communicate, sometimes expressed as a generalization about life.

Tone: The quality or feeling conveyed by the work; the author's style or manner of expression.

Lit-Circle Bibliography
GRADES THREE & FOUR

Banks, Lynn Reid. *The Indian in the Cupboard*. New York: HarperCollins, 1982.

Blume, Judy. *Tales of a Fourth Grade Nothing*. New York: Puffin, 2003. (First published in 1976.)

Byars, Betsy. *The TV Kid*. New York: Viking Press, 1976.

Cleary, Beverly. *Dear Mr. Henshaw*. New York: Morrow, 1984

Dagliesh, Alice. *The Courage of Sarah Noble*. New York: Simon and Schuster, 1986.

Dahl, Roald. *Charlie and the Chocolate Factory*. New York: Puffin, 1998. (First published in 1964.)

————. *James and the Giant Peach*. New York: Puffin, 1996. (First published in 1961.)

De Angeli, Marguerite. *The Door in the Wall*. New York: Bantam Doubleday Dell, 1990. (First published in 1949.)

Gardiner, John Reynolds. *Stone Fox*. New York: HarperCollins, 1983.

Giff, Patricia Reilly. *Lily's Crossing*. New York: Random House, 1997.

Grahame, Kenneth. *The Wind in the Willows*. New York: Dover Publications, 1999. (First published in 1940.)

Fleischman, Sid. *The Whipping Boy*. New York: Greenwillow, 1987.

Juster, Norman. *The Phantom Tollbooth*. New York: Random House, 1988. (First published in 1971.)

Lowry, Lois. *Number the Stars*. New York: Bantam Doubleday Dell, 1996.

Konigsburg, E. L. *From the Mixed-up Files of Mrs. Basil E. Frankweiler*. New York: Bantam Doubleday Dell, 1981. (First published in 1967.)

MacLachlan, Patricia. *Sarah, Plain and Tall*. New York: HarperCollins, 1986.

Naylor, Phyllis. *Shiloh*. New York: Atheneum, 1991.

O'Brien, Robert. *Mrs. Frisby and the Rats of Nimh*. New York: Aladdin, 2003. (First published in 1971.)

Paterson, Katherine. *Bridge to Terabithia*. New York: HarperCollins, 1987. (First published in 1977.)

Rockwell, Thomas. *How to Eat Fried Worms*. New York: Bantam Doubleday Dell, 1975. (First published in 1953.

Smith, Doris Buchanan. *A Taste of Blackberries*. New York: HarperCollins, 1988. (First published in 1973.)

Speare, Elizabeth. *The Sign of the Beaver*. New York: Bantam Doubleday Dell Books, 1995. (First published in 1983.)

White, E. B. *Charlotte's Web*. New York: Harper Collins, 1980. (First published 1952.)

Lit-Circle Bibliography
GRADES FIVE & SIX

Armstrong, William H. *Sounder.* New York: HarperCollins, 2001. (First published in 1969.)

Babbitt, Natalie. *Tuck Everlasting.* New York: Farrar, Straus and Giroux, 2000. First published in 1975.)

Byars, Betsy. *The Summer of the Swans.* New York: Puffin, 1981. (First published in 1970.)

Collier, James Lincoln, and Christopher Collier. *My Brother Sam Is Dead.* New York: Scholastic, 1985. (First published 1973.)

Creech, Sharon. *Walk Two Moons.* New York: HarperCollins, 1996.

Curtis, Christopher. *Bud, Not Buddy.* New York, Delacorte: 1999.

———. *The Watsons Go to Birmingham: 1963.* New York: Bantam Doubleday Dell, 1995.

Cushman, Karen. *The Midwife's Apprentice.* New York: Harper Collins, 1995.

Hesse, Karen. *Out of the Dust.* New York: Scholastic, 1997.

Konigsburg, E. L. *The View from Saturday.* New York: Simon and Schuster, 1996.

L'Engle, Madeleine. *A Wrinkle in Time.* New York: Dell, 1996. (First published in 1963.)

Lewis, C. S. *The Lion, the Witch, and the Wardrobe.* New York: Harper Collins, 1994. (First published in 1950.)

O'Dell, Scott. *Island of the Blue Dolphins.* New York: Bantam Doubleday Dell, 1971. (First published in 1960.)

———. *Sing Down the Moon.* New York: Bantam Doubleday Dell, 1992.

Park, Linda Sue. *A Single Shard.* New York: Random House, 2001.

Paterson, Katherine. *The Great Gilly Hopkins.* New York: Harper Collins, 1987.

Paulson, Gary. *Hatchet.* New York: Viking Penguin, 1988.

Peck, Richard. *A Year Down Yonder.* New York: Dial, 2000.

Rowling, J. K. *Harry Potter and the Sorcerer's Stone.* New York: Scholastic, Inc., 1998.

Sachar, Louis. *Holes.* New York: Random House, 1998.

Speare, Elizabeth George. *The Sign of the Beaver.* New York: Bantam Doubleday Dell, 1984.

Taylor, Mildred. *Roll of Thunder, Hear My Cry.* New York: Puffin Books, 1991. (First published in 1950.)

Yates, Elizabeth. *Amos Fortune, Free Man.* New York: Puffin, 1989.

Lit-Circle Bibliography
GRADES SEVEN & EIGHT

Alexander, Lloyd. *The High King.* New York: Bantam Doubleday Dell, 1969.

Avi. *Crispin: The Cross of Lead.* New York: Hyperion Books for Children, 2003.

Burnford, Sheila. *The Incredible Journey.* New York: Bantam Doubleday Dell, 1996. (First published in 1961.)

Cushman, Karen. *Catherine, Called Birdy.* Boston: Houghton Mifflin,1994.

George, Jean Craighead. *Julie of the Wolves.* New York: HarperCollins, 1996. (First published in 1937.)

Forbes, Esther. *Johnny Tremain.* New York: Bantam Doubleday Dell, 1968. (First published in 1946.)

Frank, Anne. *Diary of a Young Girl.* New York: Bantam, 1997. (First published in 1953.)

Hamilton, Virginia. *The House of Dies Drear.* New York: Simon and Schuster, 1984. (First published in 1968.)

Hinton, S. E. *The Outsiders.* New York: Puffin, 1997. (First published in 1967.)

Hunt, Irene. *Across Five Aprils.* New York: Berkeley Publishing Group, 1981. (First published in 1964.)

Lee, Harper. *To Kill a Mockingbird.* New York: HarperCollins, 2002. (First published in 1961.)

Lowry, Lois. *The Giver.* Boston: Houghton Mifflin, 1993.

Neville, Emily. *It's Like This, Cat.* New York: HarperCollins, 1963.

Paterson, Katherine. *Jacob Have I Loved.* New York: HarperCollins, 1980.

Peck, Robert Newton. *A Day No Pigs Would Die.* New York: Random House, 1994. (First published in 1972.)

Raskin, Ellen. *The Westing Game.* New York: Penguin, 1978.

Rawls, Wilson. *Where the Red Fern Grows.* New York: Dell Publishing, 1996. (First published in 1946.)

Rylant, Cynthia. *Missing May.* New York: Random House, 1993.

Speare, Elizabeth George. *The Witch of Blackbird Pond.* New York: Bantam Doubleday Dell, 1972. (First published 1958.)

Sperry, Armstrong. *Call It Courage.* New York: Aladdin Paperbacks, 1971. (First published in 1940.)

Steinbeck, John. *The Pearl.* New York: Penguin, 1992. (First published in 1947.)

Taylor, *The Cay.* New York: Random House, 2002. (First published in 1970.)

Tolkien, J. R. R. *The Hobbit.* Boston: Houghton Mifflin, 1997. (First published in 1937.)